AMAZING ANIMALS OF THE WORLD ③

Volume 5

Jackal, Side-Striped — Margay

GROLIER

an imprint of

SCHOLASTIC

Scholastic Library Publishing

www.scholastic.com/librarypublishing

First published 2006 by Grolier, an imprint of Scholastic Library Publishing

For information address the publisher: Grolier, Scholastic Library Publishing
90 Old Sherman Turnpike
Danbury, CT 06816

10 digit: Set ISBN: 0-7172-6179–4; Volume ISBN: 0-7172-6184–0
13 digit: Set ISBN: 978-0-7172-6179–6; Volume ISBN: 978-0-7172-6184–0

Printed and bound in the U.S.A.

Library of Congress Cataloging-in-Publications Data:
Amazing animals of the world 3.
p.cm.
Includes indexes.
Contents: v. 1. Abalone, Black–Butterfly, Giant Swallowtail -- v. 2. Butterfly, Indian Leaf–Dormouse, Garden -- v. 3. Duck, Ferruginous–Glassfish, Indian -- v. 4. Glider, Sugar–Isopod, Freshwater -- v. 5. Jackal, Side-Striped–Margay -- v. 6. Markhor–Peccary, Collared -- v. 7. Pelican, Brown–Salamander, Spotted -- v. 8. Salamander, Two Lined–Spider, Barrel -- v. 9. Spider, Common House–Tuna, Albacore -- v. 10. Tunicate, Light-Bulb–Zebra, Grevy's.
ISBN 0–7172–6179–4 (set : alk. paper) -- ISBN 0–7172–6180–8 (v. 1 : alk. paper) -- ISBN 0–7172–6181–6 (v. 2 : alk. paper) -- ISBN 0-7172-6182–4 (v. 3 : alk. paper) -- ISBN 0-7172-6183–2 (v. 4 : alk. paper) -- ISBN 0-7172-6184-0 (v. 5 : alk. paper) -- ISBN 0-7172-6185–9 (v. 6 : alk. paper) -- ISBN 0-7172-6186–7 (v. 7 : alk. paper) -- ISBN 0-7172-6187–5 (v. 8 : alk. paper) -- ISBN 0-7172-6188–3 (v. 9 : alk. paper) -- ISBN 0-7172-6189–1 (v. 10 : alk.paper)
1. Animals--Juvenile literature. I. Grolier (Firm) II. Title: Amazing animals of the world three.
QL49.A455 2006
590—dc22

2006010870

About This Set

Amazing Animals of the World 3 brings you pictures of 400 exciting creatures, and important information about how and where they live.

Each page shows just one species, or individual type, of animal. They all fall into seven main categories, or groups, of animals (classes and phylums scientifically) identified on each page with an icon (picture)—amphibians, arthropods, birds, fish, mammals, other invertebrates, and reptiles. Short explanations of what these group names mean, and other terms used commonly in the set, appear on page 4 in the Glossary.

Scientists use all kinds of groupings to help them sort out the types of animals that exist today and once wandered the earth (extinct species). *Kingdoms, classes, phylums, genus,* and *species* are among the key words here that are also explained in the Glossary.

Where animals live is important to know as well. Each of the species in this set lives in a particular place in the world, which you can see outlined on the map on each page. And in those places, the animals tend to favor a particular habitat—an environment the animal finds suitable for life—with food, shelter, and safety from predators that might eat it. There they also find ways to coexist with other animals in the area that might eat somewhat different food, use different homes, and so on.

Each of the main habitats is named on the page and given an icon, or picture, to help you envision it. The habitat names are further defined in the Glossary on page 4.

As well as being part of groups like species, animals fall into other categories that help us understand their lives or behavior. You will find these categories in the Glossary on page 4, where you will learn about carnivores, herbivores, and other types of animals.

And there is more information you might want about an animal—its size, diet, where it lives, and how it carries on its species—the way it creates its young. All these facts and more appear in the data boxes at the top of each page.

Finally, the set is arranged alphabetically by the most common name of the species. That puts most beetles, for example, together in a group so you can compare them easily.

But some animals' names are not so common, and they don't appear near others like them. For instance, the chamois is a kind of goat or antelope. To find animals that are similar—or to locate any species—look in the Index at the end of each book in the set (pages 45–48). It lists all animals by their various names (you will find the Giant South American River Turtle under Turtle, Giant South American River, and also under its other name— Arrau). And you will find all birds, fish, and so on gathered under their broader groupings.

Similarly, smaller like groups appear in the Set Index as well—butterflies include swallowtails and blues, for example.

Table of Contents
Volume 5

Glossary

Amphibians—species usually born from eggs in water or wet places, which change (metamorphose) into land animals. Frogs and salamanders are typical. They breathe through their skin mainly and have no scales.

Arctic and Antarctic—icy, cold, dry areas at the ends of the globe that lack trees but see small plants grown in thawed areas (tundra). Penguins and seals are common inhabitants.

Arthropods—animals with segmented bodies, hard outer skin, and jointed legs, such as spiders and crabs.

Birds—born from eggs, these creatures have wings and often can fly. Eagles, pigeons, and penguins are all birds, though penguins cannot fly through the air.

Carnivores—they are animals that eat other animals. Many species do eat each other sometimes, and a few eat dead animals. Lions kill their prey and eat it, while vultures clean up dead bodies of animals.

Cities, Towns, and Farms—places where people live and have built or used the land and share it with many species. Sometimes these animals live in human homes or just nearby.

Class—part or division of a phylum.

Deserts—dry, often warm areas where animals often are more active on cooler nights or near water sources. Owls, scorpions, and jack rabbits are common in American deserts.

Endangered—some animals in this set are marked as endangered because it is possible they will become extinct soon.

Extinct—these species have died out altogether for whatever reason.

Family—part of an order.

Fish—water animals (aquatic) that typically are born from eggs and breathe through gills. Trout and eels are fish, though whales and dolphins are not (they are mammals).

Forests and Mountains—places where evergreen (coniferous) and leaf-shedding (deciduous) trees are common, or that rise in elevation to make cool, separate habitats. Rain forests are different. (see Rain forests)

Fresh Water—lakes, rivers, and the like carry fresh water (unlike Oceans and Shores, where the water is salty). Fish and birds abound, as do insects, frogs, and mammals.

Genus—part of a family.

Grasslands—habitats with few trees and light rainfall. Grasslands often lie between forests and deserts, and they are home to birds, coyotes, antelope, and snakes, as well as many other kinds of animals.

Herbivores—these animals eat mainly plants. Typically they are hoofed animals (ungulates) that are common on grasslands, such as antelope or deer. Domestic (nonwild) ones are cows and horses.

Hibernators—species that live in harsh areas with very cold winters slow down their functions then and sort of sleep through the hard times.

Invertebrates—animals that lack backbones or internal skeletons. Many, such as insects and shrimp, have hard outer coverings. Clams and worms are also invertebrates.

Kingdom—the largest division of species. Commonly there are understood to be five kingdoms: animals, plants, fungi, protists, and monerans.

Mammals—these creatures usually bear live young and feed them on milk from the mother. A few lay eggs (monotremes like the platypus) or nurse young in a pouch (marsupials like opossums and kangaroos).

Migrators—some species spend different seasons in different places, moving to where more food, warmth, or safety can be found. Birds often do this, sometimes over long distances, but other types of animals also move seasonally, including fish and mammals.

Oceans and Shores—seawater is salty, often deep, and huge. In it live many fish, invertebrates, and even some mammals, such as whales. On the shore, birds and other creatures often gather.

Order—part of a class.

Phylum—part of a kingdom.

Rain forests—here huge trees grow among many other plants helped by the warm, wet environment. Thousands of species of animals also live in these rich habitats.

Reptiles—these species have scales, lungs to breathe, and lay eggs or give birth to live young. Dinosaurs are thought to have been reptiles, while today the class includes turtles, snakes, lizards, and crocodiles.

Scientific name—the genus and species name of a creature in Latin. For instance, Canis lupus is the wolf. Scientific names avoid the confusion possible with common names in any one language or across languages.

Species—a group of the same type of living thing. Part of an order.

Subspecies—a variant but quite similar part of a species.

Territorial—many animals mark out and defend a patch of ground as their home area. Birds and mammals may call quite small or quite large spots their territories.

Vertebrates—animals with backbones and skeletons under their skins

Side-Striped Jackal
Canis adustus

Length of the Body: about 2½ feet
Weight: 18 to 22 pounds
Diet: insects and other small animals, berries, and carcasses

Length of the Tail: about 10 inches
Number of Young: 3 to 6
Home: Africa
Order: Carnivores
Family: Dogs

 Forests and Mountains

 Mammals

© MARTIN HARVEY / GALLO IMAGES / CORBIS

Jackals are the coyotes of Africa. There are three species: the side-striped, the golden, and the black-backed jackal. All three species can be found throughout sub-Saharan Africa, but they each live in a different habitat. For the most part, the side-striped jackal prefers to live in the forest. It leaves the savannas and deserts to its cousins. The side-striped is recognized by its gray fur, the white tip of fur on its tail, and the stripes on its sides.

In lifestyle the three species are very much alike. Although they are sometimes accused of attacking livestock, jackals are more likely to eat arthropods such as millipedes, crickets, and grasshoppers. They also snack on berries and fallen fruits.

Occasionally jackals kill reptiles and small or young mammals. The jackal's own enemies include wolves, African hunting dogs, and other, larger wild dogs. Eagles sometimes kill the jackal's pups.

Side-striped jackals use caves and rock crevices for shelter. Occasionally they dig their own burrows in soft earth. Typically each burrow is occupied by a mated pair and their young. The pups are usually independent when they are eight weeks old, but they often stay with their parents for more than a year. Like coyotes, jackals love to yip and howl. Their nighttime concerts are most frequent in November and December, which is when they mate.

Arizona Jaguar
Panthera onca arizonensis

Length: 3½ to 6 feet
Length of the Tail: 1½ to 2 feet
Weight: 70 to 250 pounds
Diet: small rodents, birds, reptiles, fish, deer, and cattle

Number of Young: 1 to 4
Home: Arizona, Mexico, and Panama
Order: Carnivores
Family: Cats

 Deserts

 Mammals

© LUKE HUNTER / LONELY PLANET IMAGES

? Endangered Animals

The Arizona jaguar has the northernmost range of the five subspecies of jaguar. At one time, it roamed throughout the arid regions of the southern United States. Today, sadly, the Arizona jaguar may be extinct. No one has seen the creature in more than 20 years. The jaguars of Central and South America are close to extinction as well. Farmers and ranchers have hunted this wildcat relentlessly for hundreds of years, because it sometimes kills livestock. People have also hunted jaguars simply for the sport, keeping the cat's beautiful spotted pelt as a trophy.

The Arizona jaguar is the largest, most powerful wildcat in the Western Hemisphere. Its compact body, its stout, round legs, and its broad paws make the jaguar a strong swimmer with great endurance. Arizona jaguars prefer to live near riverbanks where they can fish and bathe. When catching fish, they pounce, much like a house cat after a mouse. Also like a house cat, jaguars are clever. They have even been seen using the tips of their tails as fishing lures, twitching them lightly over the surface of the water.

Although the Arizona jaguar may already be lost, the future for jaguars elsewhere is not hopeless. Today it is illegal to sell or bring a jaguar pelt into the United States. Costa Rica and other countries are establishing large wildlife preserves where these wildcats can roam in safety.

European Jay
Garrulus glandarius

Length: about 13 inches
Weight: about 5 ounces
Diet: insects and other invertebrates, seeds, and berries
Number of Young: 5 or 6

Home: Europe, Asia, and northern Africa
Order: Perching birds
Family: Crows, jays, and magpies

 Forests and Mountains

Birds

© NIALL BENVIE / CORBIS

The European jay looks quite unlike the familiar blue jay of North America. Although both are exceptionally handsome birds, the European jay's pinkish-brown plumage makes much better camouflage than the bright blue feathers and head cap of its American cousin. In personality the two species are more similar. Both are "talkative" songbirds that gather in noisy flocks. "Skraaaak!" screams the European jay as its voice penetrates its forest home. European jays also chuckle, click, and mew—much like mockingbirds.

Originally a woodland bird, the European jay has adapted well to civilization and often lives in parks and wooded gardens. At breeding time in the spring, the jays retreat to more secluded places. After mating, each pair disappears into the woods to build a nest. The female incubates the eggs while her mate stays nearby to guard her and to supply food. The eggs hatch after 16 to 19 days. Usually the female remains on the nest until the hatchlings are several days old. Then she helps her mate fetch insects and worms for their young.

When they are old enough to leave the nest, the fledglings join their parents in search of food. Young jays eat a variety of small creatures, including insects, spiders, slugs, snails, and worms. Adults also eat berries and grain, and can crack open acorns to get at the tasty nutmeat inside.

Lion's Mane Jellyfish
Cyanea capillata

Diameter: up to 8 feet
Length of the Tentacles: up to 200 feet
Diet: fish and other animals
Method of Reproduction: egg layer

Home: colder regions of the Atlantic and Pacific oceans and nearby seas
Order: Semaeostomes
Family: Cyaneids

 Oceans and Shores

 Other Invertebrates

© STUART WESTMORLAND / CORBIS

The lion's mane is the largest jellyfish in the world. The jellylike umbrella, or body, of some lion's manes is only 5 inches in diameter. But other specimens have umbrellas that are 8 feet across, with yellowish, 200-foot-long tentacles that somewhat resemble the flowing mane of an African lion. A lion's mane jellyfish equipped with such enormous tentacles can weigh nearly a ton. It is not surprising that another, less complimentary name for this species is "sea blubber."

The hundreds of tentacles hang downward from the umbrella or spread outward in a circle. When the jellyfish swims through the sea, its tentacles extend behind the umbrella. The highly sensitive tentacles are armed with stinging cells called nematocysts. When an animal brushes against the tentacles, the nematocysts are discharged and inject poison into the prey, disabling it. The tentacles then carry the victim to the mouth, which is on the underside of the umbrella.

Lion's manes that live in the southern part of the species' range are the smallest specimens. The giants live in cold Arctic waters. This is fortunate: imagine swimming in water where you might come in contact with such creatures! Even stings from small specimens can cause burning, muscle cramps, and breathing problems.

Melon Jellyfish
Beroe sp.

Length: up to 6 inches
Diet: small marine animals
Method of Reproduction: egg layer

Home: all oceans
Order: Active-swimming comb jellyfishes
Family: Melon comb jellyfishes

 Oceans and Shores

 Other Invertebrates

© NORBERT WU / MINDEN PICTURES

The melon jellyfish resembles one-half of a tiny, see-through watermelon. The open, or flat, end of the melon jellyfish is its large mouth. With a mouth as wide as its entire body, this creature can eat soft marine animals almost as large as itself. The melon jellyfish's thin flesh varies in color from pink to milky white. Its stripes are actually a network of canals inside its hollow, helmet-shaped body. The canals help carry nutrients from the jellyfish's food to its body.

The melon jellyfish is not a true jellyfish; it is a comb jelly. Comb jellies are named for the long rows of stiff hairs, or "combs," on their body. In order to swim, the comb jelly must constantly whir and beat the tiny comb hairs through the water. The melon jellyfish has eight comb rows that divide its body into eight equal parts. As they whir, the hairs appear to glow and shimmer. This effect is created by light-producing organs in the jellyfish's stomach. Creatures such as comb jellies that can produce their own light are called "bioluminescent."

The melon jellyfish is a hermaphrodite, which means it is both male and female at the same time. Eggs and sperm develop inside the creature's long stomach canals. They are then shed into the water, where they mix. The fertilized eggs of the melon jellyfish float among the plankton and hatch in the ocean currents.

Killdeer
Charadrius vociferus

Length: 9 to 11 inches
Weight: about 3 ounces
Home: Canada, United States, Mexico, West Indies, Peru, and Chile

Diet: insects
Number of Eggs: 4
Order: Water birds
Family: Plovers and lapwings

 Cities, Towns, and Farms

 Birds

© DARRELL / GULIN / CORBIS

The killdeer is a plover that gets its name from its call—a loud, noisy "kill-dee" that is repeated over and over again. The bird also makes trills and other sounds. In addition to its call, the adult killdeer can be recognized by the two black bands on its neck.

Killdeer live in open spaces such as pastures and farms. The birds often follow farmers plowing their fields, landing to feed on beetle grubs (larvae) that are exposed as the plows turn the soil. Killdeer also live in backyards and stone quarries, along highways and airport runways, on riverbanks and shores, and almost anywhere else that is not too far from water. They usually live in flocks of up to 50 birds. Those in areas with cold winters migrate to warmer climates in the fall.

A female killdeer lays her eggs on the ground, in a shallow nest lined with pebbles, grasses, and weeds. Both parents incubate the four eggs and care for the young. If a predator approaches, the parent killdeer will hop away from the nest, pretending to be injured. It will drag its wings on the ground, as if it were badly hurt. This distracts the predator, who forgets about the nest and follows the parent. When the predator is safely away from the nest, the parent stops pretending and suddenly flies off.

Kinkajou
Potos flavus

Length of the Body: 28 inches
Length of the Tail: 22 inches
Weight: 10 pounds
Diet: fruit, insects, and honey
Number of Young: 1 or 2

Home: Central America and northern South America
Order: Carnivores
Family: Raccoons and relatives

 Rain forests

Mammals

© MICHAEL & PATRICIA FOGDEN / CORBIS

If you were to stand in the Central American rain forest late at night, you might hear a high-pitched scream far in the distance. If you were brave enough to investigate, you would likely find the kinkajou. No horrible beast, this wide-eyed jungle gymnast is an unusual mammal about the size of a cat.

The kinkajou has quite a sweet tooth. Its favorite food is fruit, but it also loves honey. It will stick its long tongue into a beehive to slurp up the treat. The kinkajou sleeps in hollow trees by day. This is also where it gives birth to young. Newborn kinkajous cannot open their eyes for the first week. But by the end of their second month, they are eating solid food and hanging by their tails.

The kinkajou owes its gymnastic ability to its ankles, which are designed in a way that allows the feet to swivel 180 degrees. The animal can also use its long tail like an extra arm. So if a kinkajou sees a piece of fruit high above it, the kinkajou can swivel around and stretch out its tail to grab the fruit. The animal can even climb up its own tail as if it were a rope!

Scientists have had a difficult time deciding just what kind of animal the kinkajou is. Its love of honey has led some people to call it a bear. The way it swings from trees fooled some biologists into thinking the kinkajou was a primate, like monkeys. But we now know that the kinkajou is actually a relative of the raccoon.

Komodo Dragon
Varanus komodoensis

Diet: small mammals and rotting meat
Number of Eggs: approximately 25
Length: up to 11½ feet

Weight: up to 220 pounds
Home: Komodo, Flores, and nearby islands of Indonesia
Order: Lizards and snakes
Family: Monitor lizards

 Rain forests

 Reptiles

© STEPHEN FRINK / CORBIS

Endangered Animals

Do dragons really exist? The pilot who, in 1910, landed on the island of Komodo in Indonesia must have wondered. What he saw was a 10-foot-long lizard poking its forked tongue out and hissing at him! In spite of its name, the Komodo dragon is not a dragon. It does not breathe fire, and it is far from powerful. The legend soon gave way to reality: the Komodo dragon had to be protected from hunters who were after its beautiful scaly skin or captured the giant lizard for zoos. It survived, but in much smaller numbers. There are only about 7,200 Komodo dragons left on Komodo, nearby Flores, and four other smaller islands.

When the Komodo dragon hunts, it hides in high grass and waits for a deer, a goat, or a wild boar. The dragon grabs its prey; and when the prey is weak, the dragon throws it down and kills it with several bites. It prefers to hunt sick or wounded animals because they are easier to catch. It also eats dead animals. According to some observers, a 60- to 90-pound animal can be gobbled up in 15 minutes.

In spite of its size, weight, and large clawed feet, the Komodo dragon can run at a speed of 12 miles per hour. It makes very clear paths through the forest, jungle, or savanna. A good swimmer, it loves water holes and the nearby sea. Its den, usually found near the water, is a huge hole dug in the ground, in the tangle of a large tree's roots.

Banded Krait
Bungarus fasciatus

Length: 4 to 7 feet
Number of Eggs: 6 to 10
Home: northeastern India, Indochina, and the Malay Peninsula

Diet: frogs, toads, lizards, and small snakes
Order: Lizards and snakes
Family: Cobras and their relatives

 Grasslands

 Reptiles

© DAVID M. DENNIS / ANIMALS ANIMALS / EARTH SCENES

The banded krait is a peace-loving exception in a family of vicious and deadly snakes. Among its ill-tempered cousins are the king cobra and the death adder. Yet the banded krait seldom strikes at humans—even when accidentally disturbed. But do not temp fate; this snake produces one of the most toxic venoms in the world.

The banded krait's venom is a powerful nerve poison that can kill a victim by stopping its heartbeat and breathing. As with other venomous serpents, this snake's poison comes from its salivary glands. The deadly drool runs down grooves on the back of the krait's fangs. The grooves meet to form a tube (much like the syringe of a needle) that ends at the tip of each fang.

The banded krait usually kills its prey by injecting venom as it chews.

This reptile spends most of its day hidden under stones or fallen trees. It emerges at nightfall and slithers through the fields and meadows—never venturing too far from a pond or stream. It devours frogs, lizards, and other snakes unfortunate enough to cross its path.

Like many poisonous snakes, the banded krait is easy to recognize. Its glossy yellow and black bands serve to warn predators not to attack. All species of krait have a ridge running along the top of their body, from their small, flat head to their pointed tail. The banded krait also has a black arrow-shaped mark on top of its head.

Yellow-Lipped Sea Krait
Laticauda colubrina

Length: 24 to 55 inches
Home: tropical coasts of eastern Indian Ocean and western Pacific Ocean

Diet: mainly eels
Number of Eggs: 4 to 6
Order: Lizards and snakes
Family: Sea snakes

  Oceans and Shores

Reptiles

© FRED BAVENDAM / PETER ARNOLD, INC.

There are about 50 species of snakes that live in the sea. Most of them never leave the water. Sea kraits are an exception to the rule, dividing their time between the sea and dry land. Just after dusk the krait dives into coastal waters to catch its favorite food—eels. Occasionally it also eats small fish. At dawn the krait slithers back to shore. After sunning itself briefly, the snake seeks shelter in warm rocks or in a patch of thick beach vegetation. Sea kraits also rest in the crevices of exposed coral reefs. Females leave their eggs under palm fronds and fallen branches.

The yellow-lipped sea krait is named for the bright color of its snout and upper lip.

The rest of its body is circled by alternating bands of black and bluish gray or brown. Like other sea snakes, the krait's tail is shaped like a flattened paddle. This enables the krait to move quickly through the water. Sea kraits can also travel well on land, while other types of sea snakes are quite awkward out of water.

The venom of the sea krait can be lethal and has even been compared to that of the deadly Indian cobra. However, sea kraits bite only to kill prey. Reportedly, they never strike humans—even when handled. The American snake expert Charles Pope once wrote of sea kraits: "They are at once the most venomous and the most harmless of poisonous snakes." Still, caution is advised!

Two-Spot Ladybug
Adalia bipunctata

Length: ⅛ to ¼ inch
Home: North and South America, Europe, and Great Britain

Diet: aphids
Number of Eggs: up to 800
Order: Beetles
Family: Ladybugs

 Cities, Towns, and Farms

 Arthropods

© HOLT STUDIOS / NIGEL CATTLIN / PHOTO RESEARCHERS

In the spring and summer, two-spot ladybugs decorate our meadows, fields, and gardens. In fall and winter, they can often be found indoors. These pretty little beetles have been known to hibernate by the thousands inside garages, basements, or hollow walls. Most two-spot ladybugs, called ladybirds in England, have light red wing covers, or elytra. But some are darkly colored, and others have more than two spots.

In spring, the female two-spot ladybug lays her eggs on a leaf. In about a week, the eggs hatch into velvety black larvae with yellow and white spots. As they quickly grow, the larvae molt (shed their skin) four times in one or two months. After the fourth molt, the larva dangles its body off the edge of a leaf and becomes very still. In this stage the insect is called a pupa. In six to nine days, it reawakens as an adult.

Two-spot ladybugs are loved not only for their beauty. These insects are a great help to people. The ladybugs love to eat aphids—tiny green insect pests that attack plants. There are some 3,000 other species of ladybugs in the world. Most, but not all, eat insect pests. During the Middle Ages, when ladybugs saved European vineyards from insect pests, the beetles were gratefully dedicated to "Our Lady," Saint Mary. And that is how they got their name.

Brook Lamprey
Lampetra planeri

Length: 5 to 8 inches
Diet: organic matter
Home: Europe and
    northwestern Asia

Number of Eggs: 600 to 1,500
Order: Lampreys
Family: Lampreys

 Fresh Water

 Fish

© MICHEL RIBETTE / BIOS / PETER ARNOLD, INC.

Most lampreys are parasites that attach themselves to other fish by means of a round, sucking mouth. They then proceed to suck out the blood and body fluids of their victims. But adult brook lampreys do not eat at all. They only have one purpose: to reproduce. Within a few weeks after the eggs are laid and fertilized, the parents die.

Brook-lamprey eggs hatch into tiny larvae called ammocoetes. The ammocoetes do not look at all like their parents. In fact, at one time scientists thought they were an entirely different kind of animal. An ammocoete is a blind, toothless creature with a horseshoe-shaped mouth. The mouth has a screenlike structure that filters particles of organic

matter from the water. Immediately after hatching, the ammocoetes burrow into the mud or sand at the bottom of a stream so that hungry fish will not find and eat them. The ammocoetes stay in the burrows they have dug with only their heads uncovered, to get food. If they sense danger, they quickly duck out of sight.

The ammocoete phase lasts about four years. Then the creature slowly changes, or metamorphoses, into an adult. The mouth becomes rounder, and teeth begin to form. Eyes and other adult organs develop. The body color changes. When metamorphosis is complete, the brook lamprey mates, stops eating, and its digestive system wastes away. It soon dies.

Lancelet (Amphioxus)
Branchiostoma sp.

Length: ½ to 4 inches
Diet: plankton and dissolved food particles
Method of Reproduction: egg layer

Height: about ¼ inch
Home: coasts of Pacific and Atlantic oceans
Order: Copelata
Family: Lancelets

 Oceans and Shores

 Other Invertebrates

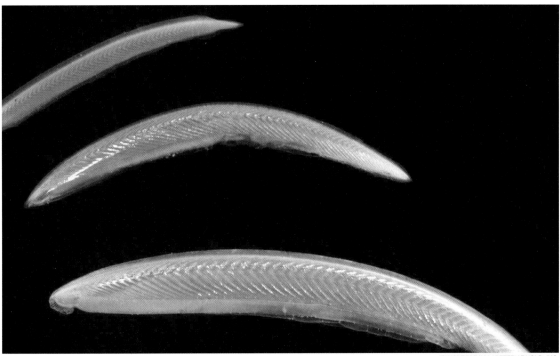

At first glance, you might mistake the lancelet for a minnow. But this is no fish. Close examination reveals that this creature has no head! Nor does it have a brain, heart, or spine. The lancelet is a primitive creature that burrows into the sand in shallow seawater. The front tip of its body sticks out of the sand, revealing a simple mouth filled with tiny hairs and tentacles. The lancelet pumps water into its mouth and out of its primitive gills. In this way, it filters tiny bits of food from the water. When disturbed, lancelets can jump out of the sand and swim rapidly away.

Most lancelets belong to the genus *Branchiostoma* and are sometimes called amphioxi. They are caught in large numbers by the Chinese, who serve them for dinner. Most are about two inches long.

These simple creatures are of great interest to scientists. Evolutionary biologists believe that all vertebrate animals—from fish to dinosaurs to humans—are descended from a creature very much like the lancelet, or amphioxus.

Although it is an invertebrate (an animal without a backbone), the lancelet has a primitive spinal cord called a notochord. The notochord may have been the evolutionary starting point of the world's first backbone…and so gave rise to all the world's vertebrate animals.

Norway Lemming
Lemmus lemmus

Length: 5 to 6 inches
Diet: lichens, mosses, and grasses
Number of Young: 4 to 15

Home: northern Europe
Order: Rodents
Family: Rats and mice

Arctic and Anarctic

Mammals

© SOLVIN ZANKL / FOTO NATURA / MINDEN PICTURES

The Norway lemming looks like a field mouse. It lives in the tundra, a plain near the always frozen Arctic Circle. It spends the summer in wet regions where the dwarf trees grow. In the fall, it lives in drier places. It spends the winter in nests and tunnels it makes under the snow. It eats mainly lichens, mosses, and grasses. Lemmings have many offspring, even during the winter.

In 1532, reports on the strange behavior of this little rodent began to appear. Large numbers of lemmings were said to be moving toward the sea. These animals jumped into the water and drowned in what looked like a mass suicide. Other witnesses said that lemmings rained from the sky during a storm! Today we know it is true that the lemming runs away from its original territory to control its population. This behavior is tied to weather conditions and the lemming's nature. It is no longer believed that the lemmings commit suicide. While some lemmings may try to cross rivers or fiords, very few ever reach the sea.

There is a large increase in the number of lemmings from time to time. Although no one knows exactly why, scientists have some ideas. One idea is that more lemmings are born and survive when the weather is good for several seasons in a row. Perhaps vitamins in the lichens the lemmings eat may trigger changes in the way they mate and grow.

Black Lemur
Lemur macaco

Length of the Body: 14 to 16 inches
Length of the Tail: 18 to 20 inches
Weight: 4½ to 6½ pounds

Diet: fruits and insects
Number of Young: 1 or 2
Home: northern Madagascar
Order: Primates
Family: Lemurs

 Rain forests

 Mammals

? Endangered Animals

© PATTI MURRAY / ANIMALS ANIMALS / EARTH SCENES

The black lemur's name is somewhat confusing because the adult female is a rusty red. Her mate is black, as are their young. The female turns reddish brown when she is about six months old. The word *lemur* is Latin for "ghost." The lemurs are named for their spooky nighttime voices and their large eyes, which shine in the dark.

The loud screams made by a black lemur family can be quite scary. Each family consists of about 10 individuals, including several adults and children of different ages. Their screams and cries warn other lemur families to respect their territory. Members of the group also mark their "property" by rubbing their legs against trees and rocks. This leaves a unique family scent.

Black lemurs are especially good jumpers. They can leap as far as 26 feet from one high branch to another, while seldom descending from the treetops. When not grazing on fruits and insects, the lemurs spend hours lazily grooming their fur. They use their claws like combs to remove small bits of skin and dirt.

Like all lemurs the black species is in danger of extinction. Its habitat is growing smaller as humans continue to cut down the rain forest of Madagascar. Black lemurs live in the deepest, darkest parts of the undisturbed rain forest, but there are fewer and fewer of these places left.

Mongoose Lemur
Lemur mongoz

Length of the Body: about 17 inches

Length of the Tail: about 17 inches

Diet: fruits, flowers, leaves, and other plant matter

Weight: about 4½ pounds

Number of Young: usually 1

Home: northern Madagascar

Order: Primates

Family: Lemurs

 Rain forests

© ALAN D. CAREY / PHOTO RESEARCHERS

Mammals

Endangered Animals

The mongoose lemur looks much like the darkly colored mongoose of India. Both have a sharp snout and a long, heavy tail. The lemur is a patchwork of colors, with dark gray fur on the head and shoulders, a reddish neck, and a brown back. Its snout, throat, and chest are noticeably lighter. Males and females look quite different. The male has a reddish-yellow belly and a reddish-brown tail. The female's face and tail are black, and her underparts are white. The lemur keeps its long fur immaculately groomed, using its tongue, teeth, and grooming claws as preening tools.

All true lemurs live on Madagascar and surrounding islands. The mongoose species is found in the jungle of northern Madagascar, an area that has been greatly disturbed by the island's human population. While some species of lemur have adapted to civilization, the mongoose lemur has not. It quickly moves on when humans intrude. Making matters worse, farmers shoot, trap, and poison lemurs, which they accuse of stealing their crops. Between hunting and habitat destruction, the lemur has been driven to the brink of extinction.

The lemur prefers to remain in the dense rain forest, where it lives in peaceful family groups of six to eight adults and their young. The mothers within the group provide "baby-sitting" services. Thus lemur young are accustomed to nursery life.

Sportive Lemur
Lepilemur mustelinus

Length: 10 to 12 inches (19 to 21 inches with tail)
Diet: mainly leaves
Number of Young: 1

Home: Madagascar
Order: Primates
Family: Lemurs

 Rain forests

 Mammals

© WENDY DENNIS / VISUALS UNLIMITED

Endangered Animals

During the day, the sportive lemur curls up and sleeps in a hollow tree or in thick bushes. At dusk, it starts moving around. It has large eyes that help it see well at night. When it is on the ground, it hops on its hind legs like a kangaroo. It jumps easily from one tree trunk to another and stops from time to time to nibble on a flower or a juicy leaf.

Sportive lemurs live in the forests of Madagascar, a large island off the eastern coast of Africa. They spend almost as much time watching their territory as they do looking for food. Usually they live alone or in pairs. Each lemur's territory covers only ½ to 1 acre of land. The lemur climbs to the top of trees to watch its neighbors. Look out for any lemur that wants part of

another's territory! Males as well as females may fight each other. They make screeching sounds to scare their opponents away. Usually, one animal breaks down and goes away.

The mating season lasts from May to August. The female gives birth to a single offspring about 4½ months later. In a nest hidden in a tree trunk, the young sportive lemur waits for one of its parents to bring it food. It starts to eat leaves after it is 4 months old, and lives on its own when it is one year old. Humans came to Madagascar thousands of years ago and have changed the environment dramatically. Lemurs and other native animals are almost all endangered as a result.

Clouded Leopard
Neofelis nebulosa

Length of the Body: 2½ to
  3½ feet
Length of the Tail: 2 to 3 feet
Weight: 37 to 55 pounds
Diet: birds, monkeys, pigs,
  cattle, goats, and deer

Number of Young: 2 to 4
Home: southern Asia and
  Taiwan
Order: Carnivores
Family: Cats

Rain forests

Mammals

Endangered
Animals

© TOM BRAKEFIELD / CORBIS

The clouded leopard is one of the most beautiful creatures in the animal kingdom. Its striking coat is a pattern of black curving stripes that form large squares and rectangles across the yellowish fur. Within each square are many faded spots. The leopard's long tail sways gracefully as the animal moves. And when the cat opens its mouth, another distinguishing feature is visible—four long fangs. The leopard roars very much like a tiger, but it can also purr like a domestic house cat.

The clouded leopard lives across a wide expanse of southern Asia, where it is at home in the tropical jungle and in the cool evergreen rain forests at the foot of the Himalaya Mountains. The cat is an expert climber and can even shinny down tall trees headfirst. In fact the leopard spends more time in the trees than do most wildcats. In captivity, scientists have witnessed females giving birth in the trees.

Because the clouded leopard spends so much of its life in the trees, scientists have not been able to keep track of the animal's population. All hope that the species is more common than it appears to be. Yet there is little doubt that the leopard is in great danger of extinction. People have hunted the animal for its luxurious fur, and its home—the tropical rain forest—is slowly dying. Many governments have banned the import of the leopards' pelts.

Pellucid Limpet
Patina pellucida

Length: ¾ inch
Diet: plants
Method of Reproduction: egg layer

Home: northeastern Atlantic Ocean
Order: Primitive snails
Family: Limpets

Oceans and Shores

Other Invertebrates

The word *pellucid* means "shining," "iridescent," and "pleasing in appearance." These words well describe the tiny but beautiful pellucid limpet. This shellfish, a small relative of the abalone, is loveliest when it is young. The young pellucid's shell is smooth and translucent, with vivid, shimmering blue stripes. As the pellucid limpet ages, its shell becomes thicker and loses its pretty blue rays.

You will find pellucid limpets on only one specific type of kelp, a sea plant called *laminaria*. The young limpets live on the kelp's fronds, or leaves. The older, larger limpets live on the kelp's stalk, or stem. The limpets eat the kelp by scraping the plant's surface with their rough tongue, called a "radula." Like all snails the pellucid's tongue is at the bottom of its single foot.

Many pellucid limpets are destroyed when humans harvest laminaria kelp. Pellucids also have many natural predators, such as sea stars, octopuses, and meat-eating fish. Fortunately, this lovely limpet reproduces easily. Male and female pellucids spray large amounts of eggs and sperm into the water. The fertilized eggs hatch into tiny larvae, or immature limpets. The larvae have a round body ringed with even, tiny hairs called cilia. Whirring their cilia, the larvae paddle through the water. In their first few months of life, the larvae grow rapidly and undergo many body changes. Eventually they attach to kelp and grow their adult shell.

Limpkin
Aramus guarauna

Length: 23 to 28 inches
Wingspan: 42 inches
Weight: 2 to 2¾ pounds
Diet: snails, mussels, and other small animals
Number of Eggs: 4 to 8

Home: southeastern United States, Central America, and South America
Order: Cranes and rails
Family: Limpkins

 Fresh Water

 Birds

© ERIC AND DAVID HOSKING / CORBIS

Many nights in the swamp, the quiet is broken by what sounds like a crying child. Soon many crying children can be heard. Fortunately, the noises are not the cries of children, but rather the sounds of limpkins. The loud wails are so similar to human cries that some people call limpkins "crying birds."

Limpkins are named for the awkward lurching way in which they move—almost as if they were limping. They have long legs, long toes, a long neck, and a bill twice as long as the head. As a limpkin walks along, it often pokes its bill into the mud to grab snails and other small aquatic animals. Sometimes the limpkin rests on trees or bushes at the edge of a marsh. From this perch the bird can look around, watching for frogs or other prey. If something disturbs the limpkin, it flies off. In flight, its neck is extended, and its legs dangle downward. It stays close to the ground as it flies.

Unlike many birds, limpkins do not migrate as the seasons change. They live in the same area throughout the year. There they build their nests in trees or bushes or just above the water in a marsh. The nest is a sturdy platform of dried grasses, where the female can lay her eggs undisturbed by predators. Both parents take turns incubating, or sitting on, the eggs. Young limpkins are well developed at birth, and they leave the nest the day they hatch.

Linnet
Acanthis cannabina

Length: 5 inches
Diet: seeds
Home: Europe and North Africa

Number of Eggs: 4 to 6
Order: Perching birds
Family: Finches

 Grasslands

 Birds

© MARTIN WOIKE / FOTO NATURA / MINDEN PICTUES

If you are in Europe between March and July and take a walk in the countryside, you may hear the musical song of a group of linnets as they hop around in the fields. This bird used to be put in cages and in birdhouses for the soft and melodious quality of its singing. Its trills have been said to be as harmonious as those of the nightingale.

Linnets live in groups that sometimes contain several hundred birds. They hop tirelessly across pastures, heaths, or cultivated fields looking for seeds on the ground or on plants.

In Europe, people use the expression "linnet head" to describe an absent-minded person. It comes from the fact that the linnet often builds its nest in an exposed place that is easy for predators to spot. One pair of linnets often builds its nest next to that of another pair, but fights are rare. Linnets build their nests in a bush or on the ground, in a tuft of grass or under a rock. From April until about August, linnets lay four to six eggs twice. The eggs hatch 10 to 12 days later. After the second group of young is hatched, the parents and the young join older linnets in fields that have just been harvested. In September or October, linnets that have spent the summer in northern or eastern Europe migrate to southern Europe. In the cold regions of the north and the east, the soft melodious song of the linnet is not heard again until spring.

Bush Lizard
Polychrus marmoratus

Length: 12 to 20 inches
Diet: mainly insects
Method of Reproduction: egg layer

Home: South America
Order: Lizards and snakes
Family: Iguanas

  Rain forests

Reptiles

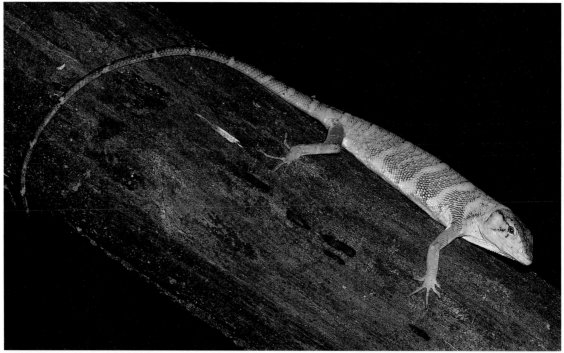

© DAVID T. ROBERTS / NATURE'S IMAGES / PHOTO RESEARCHERS

Many bush lizards are imported into the United States for the pet trade, where they are often sold under the name South American chameleon. Like the true chameleons of Eurasia and Africa, the bush lizard changes color according to its mood and temperature. A relaxed bush lizard basking on a sunny branch tends to be brown. Fighting males, on the other hand, turn a vivid green, with black patches behind their eyes.

The bush lizard is a slow-moving creature that relies on camouflage, rather than speed, to escape predators. Its enemies include large snakes and birds of prey. To avoid them the bush lizard spends most of the day hiding, perfectly still, in a shrub or bush. At night, it awakens to hunt. Bush lizards slowly stalk their prey and then snap. Their favorite foods include flies, beetles, moths, and spiders.

In nature, bush lizards seldom come down from the branches of shrubs and small trees. They are well adapted for scrambling along thin branches. Their feet are split so that some toes oppose the others. This enables the lizard to grip a branch, much as a person would grip a pole with the fingers and thumb. When the bush lizard needs some extra support, it hangs on with its long, flexible tail. When you look at a bush lizard head-on, you can see that it is very flattened from side to side. This also helps the lizard keep balanced.

Emerald Lizard
Lacerta viridis

Length: 12 to 18 inches
Diet: insects, fruits, and eggs
Number of Eggs: 5 to 20

Home: Europe
Order: Lizards and snakes
Family: Old World lizards

Cities, Towns, and Farms

Reptiles

© SUZANNE L. COLLINS / PHOTO RESEARCHERS

Emerald lizards love to be warm and dry. They do best on hillsides and high riverbanks, where there are few shade trees but lots of bushes and weeds. During mating season, emerald-lizard couples can often be seen basking together on rocks or a patch of bare ground. The male is easily recognized by his bright blue throat. The female is less colorful but also has the brilliant green scales that give this lizard its name.

The male's throat turns blue only in springtime, when he advertises his readiness to mate. When two breeding males meet, they display their blue throats and stamp toward each other with jerky steps. With great excitement, they lash their tails from side to side until one or the other signals defeat. The loser shows his submission with a special ritual called "treading." He moves his front legs rapidly up and down while staying in one place. Such a treading male is never attacked. However, if neither lizard is willing to admit defeat, a fierce battle is sure to follow. With great snapping and clawing, both emerald lizards may come away seriously injured.

Emerald lizards can be easily tamed and make excellent pets. To thrive, they need a very large, sandy cage, some rocks, and a sizable water dish. Although they prefer live insects, these attractive creatures will eat meat and raw eggs from a plate.

Flat Lizard
Platysaurus intermedius

Length: about 1 foot
Diet: locusts and beetles
Number of Eggs: 2
Home: South Africa

Order: Lizards and snakes
Family: Girdled and plated lizards

 Grasslands

 Reptiles

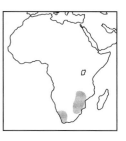

© PATRICK FAGOT / NHPA

The flat lizard is flat for a very important reason. It escapes capture from predators by squeezing its thin body into narrow rock crevices. Once inside a crack, the lizard puffs out its body and braces its legs. This makes it nearly impossible to pull out.

Flat lizards are found on only three kinds of stone—granite, paragneiss, and sandstone—because these rocks form the right kind of cracks. The lizards retreat to their cracks and crevices at nightfall, and emerge when the sun has warmed the surface of the rock.

Flat lizards live life in the slow lane. Most of the day, they can be found soaking up the rays of the strong African sun. Like all lizards, this species is cold-blooded and depends on the sun to warm its body. At midday the flat lizard takes a nap in the shade. But all the while, it keeps an eye out for insects. It will literally hurl itself at any beetle or locust that comes within reach.

In contrast to most lizards, male and female flat lizards look quite different. The male is larger and brighter. During mating season, the male defends his territory from other males and tries to attract females. He does this by arching back his head and neck to display his colorful throat and chest. Once mated, a female flat lizard produces a pair of long eggs. As you might have guessed, she shoves them into a rock crack for safekeeping.

Frilled Lizard
Chlamydosaurus kingii

Length: up to 3 feet
Diet: insects, spiders, and small mammals
Method of Reproduction: egg layer

Home: Australia and New Guinea
Order: Lizards and snakes
Family: Dragon lizards
Suborder: Lizards

 Forests and Mountains

 Reptiles

© MICHAEL & PATRICIA FOGDEN / CORBIS

The frilled lizard is one of the most spectacular lizards in the world. It is named for the large skin fold around its neck. Usually this "frill" is kept folded against the neck and shoulders, like a cape. But when an enemy approaches, and the lizard feels threatened, it expands the frill. Fully upright, the frill may have a diameter of 12 inches! It is supported by rods of cartilage. The frill makes the lizard look big and fierce. At the same time, the lizard may stand on its back legs, swing its tail back and forth, and hiss to show its teeth. If all this fails to scare the enemy, the lizard turns around and runs quickly away. Often it runs upright on its back legs, with its tail off the ground.

Frilled lizards live in woodlands and scrub areas in warm regions of Australia and New Guinea. They spend most of their time in trees. However, they descend to the ground to hunt for insects, mice, and other prey. They hunt during the daytime, using their excellent eyesight to spot prey and to avoid enemies. Their legs are well developed, and the lizards can run quickly on the ground, up tree trunks, and along branches. They use the sharp claws on their feet to grab prey.

Males also use their frills to attract females. After mating, a female lays eggs with strong, tough shells. The frill is only slightly developed when the babies hatch; it grows larger as the lizards mature.

Middle American Night Lizard
Lepidophyma flavimaculatum

Length: 8 to 12 inches
Diet: termites, ants, beetles, flies, spiders, scorpions, and centipedes

Number of Young: 1 to 3
Home: Central America
Order: Lizards and snakes
Family: Night lizards

 Rain forests

 Reptiles

© MICHAEL FOGDEN / ANIMALS ANIMALS / EARTH SCENES

The Middle American night lizard is a fearless hunter that stalks its prey after the sun goes down. During the day, it hides in caves and crevices and under logs and clumps of tropical plants. Its main foods include a wide variety of insects and spiders, including poisonous scorpions and centipedes. This species of night lizard is found only in the moist lowland jungles of Panama and Costa Rica, and the coastal regions of Nicaragua and El Salvador.

The night lizard is closely related to the gecko, another lizard with a soft, flattened body and permanently open eyes. These lizards have no eyelids. Their eyes are protected by large, transparent scales. Tiny scales cover the lizard's back and sides, and very large scales protect the belly. The toes end in long, sharp claws.

Like other night lizards, the Middle American species gives birth to live young instead of eggs. The newborns emerge from their mother tail first and usually upside down. Oddly, several populations of Middle American night lizards consist solely of females. These all-female populations live in Panama and Costa Rica. Their eggs do not need to be fertilized in order to develop into young lizards. This type of nonsexual reproduction is called *parthenogenesis* and occurs with some frequency among invertebrate animals, but rarely among lizards and higher animals.

30

Ocellated Lizard
Lacerta lepida

Length of the Body: 8 inches
Length of the Tail: up to 24 inches
Diet: insects, spiders, eggs, and occasionally fruit
Number of Eggs: 6 to 16

Home: Iberian Peninsula, France, Italy, and northwestern Africa
Order: Snakes and lizards
Family: True lizards

 Forests and Mountains

 Reptiles

© WINIFRED WISNIEWSKI / FRANK LANE PICTURE AGENCY / CORBIS

The ocellated lizard—the largest lizard in all of Europe—looks as though it has eyes behind its head . . . and down its back as well. This species gets its name from these many black-rimmed blue spots, which in scientific lingo are called ocelli, or eyespots. As you might guess, it is sometimes called the "eyed" lizard. It also deserves the name "jeweled lizard" because its blue spots glisten in the sunlight.

The ocellated lizard is a sun worshiper, even to the point of being out in the heat of midday. When it is not sunning itself, this lizard is busy hunting insects and spiders in the scrubby bushes of its arid, rocky home.

While insects are the lizard's favorite food, it may also steal eggs from birds that nest on the ground. It has even been known to eat other lizards—including its own kind. The ocellated lizard has a bad reputation among farmers as a fruit thief. Though it will nibble grapes and other sweet crops, the amount of damage is, in truth, minimal.

The ocellated lizard has learned that it is not welcome around most European farms and gardens. It is quite shy and cautious, and will quickly flee from humans—usually hiding in bushes, rabbit holes, or even the cracks of an old stone wall. However, ocellated lizards can be tamed and make good terrarium pets. They are intelligent enough to recognize their keeper and accept food only from his or her hand.

Oriental Long-Tailed Lizard
Takydromus sexlineatus

Length: 8 to 14 inches
Diet: insects and spiders
Number of Eggs: 1 to 4

Home: eastern Asia
Order: Lizards and snakes
Family: True lizards

 Grasslands

 Reptiles

© DANIEL HEUCLIN / NHPA

The oriental long-tailed lizard appears weightless as it runs across the top of a patch of tall grass. This lizard's extraordinary tail can be three to five times longer than the rest of its body. The long tail enables the lizard to spread its weight over several tall stalks without bending any of them. Although the long-tailed lizard's legs are small, they are well developed and strong. Its long and slender toes are specially designed for clinging to grasses and other stems. As the oriental long-tailed lizard leaps from one plant to the next, it uses its long, flexible tail to grab hold and balance itself.

Heavier snakes and other ground-dwelling predators find it nearly impossible to catch up with the oriental long-tailed lizard. This reptile also has the advantage of camouflage. Its brown-and-tan-striped body looks much like the grass stalks on which it lives.

The oriental long-tailed lizard is most abundant on sunny meadows and grassy slopes. It can be found in rain forest clearings as well. This lizard is lively in the morning and late afternoon, when temperatures are pleasantly warm. Like all lizards, it depends on the sun to warm its body. When the weather is cool, the long-tailed lizard has little energy to move. Lizards can also overheat easily. So at midday, this species wisely stays hidden in the shade.

Rainbow Lizard
Agama agama

Length: 12 to 16 inches
Number of Eggs: usually 3 to 8
Diet: spiders and insects

Home: Africa, the Middle East, and western Asia
Order: Lizards and snakes
Family: Dragon lizards

 Grasslands

 Reptiles

© JOE MCDONALD / CORBIS

Rainbow lizards love company! They live in family groups of up to 25 individuals, with an adult male as the leader of each group. In early morning, just after dawn, rainbow lizards come out of their nighttime hiding places and crawl onto nearby rocks, tree trunks, or walls to warm themselves in the sun.

After a while, most of the lizards move on to hunt for spiders, beetles, and other prey. Only the male leader remains, sitting in a spot where he can watch the group's territory. If a male from another group comes into the territory, the leader tries to frighten him away. If threats do not work, the two lizards fight, using their tails to hit each other on the head. Usually the leader defeats the intruder, who runs away, while the leader returns to his watching spot. As the sun sets and night begins to fall, all the members of the group gather to spend the night together.

Mating occurs during the rainy season. After two rainbow lizards mate, the female digs a small hole in moist soil. She carefully lays her eggs in the hole, then covers them with soil. The baby lizards hatch in two to three months. At first, each baby hides alone among grasses, leaves, and other plants, feeding on ants and small insects. When the rainbow lizard is several months old, it joins the family group.

Sharp-Snouted Snake Lizard
Lialis burtonis

Length: up to 2 feet
Diet: smaller lizards and insects
Method of Reproduction: egg layer

Home: Australia and New Guinea
Order: Lizards and snakes
Family: Snake lizards

Rain forests

Reptiles

© MICHAEL & PATRICIA FOGDEN / MINDEN PICTURES

At first glance, even scientists who specialize in reptiles mistake the long, legless sharp-snouted snake lizard for a true snake. But a closer look reveals a body covered with small scales of equal size. In contrast, most snakes have large, wide scales down their belly and smaller scales on top. Also, a snake lizard has two tiny external ears; true snakes have no ear openings.

The sharp-snouted snake lizard is the most widespread species of its kind. It ranges across all of Australia and eastern New Guinea, and has adapted to a wide range of habitats, from dense rain forests to dry grasslands.

Most of these lizards have distinctive cream-colored and light-brown stripes on the sides of their head and body. But individuals of this species are so variable in color and markings that no two look exactly alike.

This legless lizard is active both day and night. On bright, sunny days, it frequently hunts for smaller lizards. When it cannot find reptilian food, it reluctantly eats insects. Typically a sharp-snouted snake lizard hunts by ambush, hiding in clumps of grass or beneath dead leaves. With lightning speed, it seizes its victim by forcefully snapping shut its jaws. Snake lizards swallow their prey whole and headfirst—the same way true snakes do.

Viviparous Lizard
Lacerta vivipara

Length: up to 7 inches, including a 4-inch tail
Diet: mainly insects; also other small invertebrates
Number of Young: 4 to 10

Home: Europe and Asia
Order: Lizards and snakes
Family: Common Old World lizards

 Grasslands

 Reptiles

© DENNIS JOHNSON / PAPILIO / CORBIS

The viviparous lizard is the most common lizard in Europe. It can live in many different habitats: meadows and other open lands, at the edge of forests, and even in dense woodlands. If a predator grabs hold of the lizard's long, slender tail, it breaks off. While the predator holds the tail, the lizard runs away. Within a few months, the lizard grows a new tail.

The word "viviparous" refers to the most unusual characteristic of this lizard: it gives birth to live, well-developed young. Unfortunately, the name of this lizard is slightly in error. A viviparous animal is one that produces living young *instead* of eggs. Actually, the lizard is "ovoviviparous." It

produces eggs ("ova") that, after being fertilized, remain in the mother's body. They do not develop eggshells. The rest of the egg, including the yolk, is present within a thin, transparent membrane. The developing embryos are nourished by the yolk. It takes about three months for the embryos to develop. Then the young lizards break through the membrane and are born.

Because the viviparous lizard does not lay its eggs, the species can live in the far north of Europe and Asia. Summer is short in the far north. Lizard eggs laid in the cold ground would not survive. But temperatures inside the mother lizard remain high enough to allow the eggs to survive and develop.

Wiegmann's Burrowing Lizard
Trogonophis wiegmanni

Length: 6 to 9½ inches
Diet: ants and termites
Number of Young: 2 to 5

Home: northwestern Africa
Order: Lizards and snakes
Family: Burrowing lizards

  Grasslands

 Reptiles

© TOM MCHUGH / PHOTO RESEARCHERS

This strange, legless lizard comes out of its underground burrow only on rainy nights and when its tunnels become flooded. Although seldom seen, Wiegmann's burrowing lizard is instantly recognizable. Its wormlike body is covered with countless tiny, square scales—some light and some dark—like the squares on a chessboard.

Over the ages, Wiegmann's burrowing lizard has entirely lost the visible portions of its legs. (Inside its body are the remnants of hips and shoulders.) With no legs, a small head, and a blunt tail, the lizard has a perfectly streamlined shape. It can slide quickly backward and forward with equal ease. Evolution has even adapted the lizard's eyes for life underground. Its eyes are very tiny and covered by translucent scales that keep out the dirt.

Wiegmann's burrowing lizard spends most of the day lengthening its many tunnels with its strong snout. It burrows under anthills and termite nests, and attacks the insects from beneath. When it comes to the surface at night, the lizard usually stays near the edges of rocks and logs, where it finds more insects.

Biologists know little about the mating habits of Wiegmann's burrowing lizard. They do know that the pregnant female keeps her eggs inside her body until they hatch. She gives birth in late summer to several babies that are already quite large.

European Lobster
Homarus gammarus

Diet: sea snails, sea worms, starfish, fish, dead plants, and animals
Home: northeastern Atlantic Ocean and the Mediterranean Sea

Length: up to 20 inches
Number of Eggs: up to 30,000
Order: Shrimps, crabs, and lobsters
Family: Clawed lobsters

Oceans and Shores

Arthropods

© CLAUDE BUIHARD / BIOS / PETER ARNOLD, INC.

The European lobster is a more slender version of the American lobster, which most of us have seen on the dinner table. It is also blue, rather than the bright reddish-orange of its American cousin. Both types are a mottled white across their underside.

The European lobster likes to burrow in the soft, muddy sediment of the seafloor in shallow waters near the coast. It will also make a home out of a crack in a rock—by backing in tailfirst. With its claws sticking out of its mudhole or rock crack, the lobster stays ready to snap up a passing fish or invertebrate. Lobsters are voracious scavengers, eating just about anything they find. They grow slowly, beginning as flea-sized larvae that swim without a shell. As adults, lobsters shed their shells every year or two and grow larger ones.

Female lobsters mate right after they have shed their old shell and before they have finished growing their new one. A female's male mate must be larger than she, for he must be able to turn her over to deposit his sperm on her eggs. Once the eggs are fertilized, the female carries them under her abdomen for nearly a year. Although each female European lobster can produce more than 1,000 eggs, most of her young are eaten when they are still free-swimming larvae. Those that survive metamorphose, or change, into bug-sized adult lobsters and settle to the ocean floor.

Red-Throated Loon
Gavia stellata

Length: 24 to 27 inches
Wingspan: 42 to 45 inches
Weight: 3½ to 4 pounds
Diet: mainly fish
Number of Eggs: usually 2

Home: northern tundra and forests of North America, Europe, and Asia
Order: Loons
Family: Loons

 Fresh Water

 Birds

© MICHAEL CALLAN / FRANK LANE PICTURE AGENCY / CORBIS

The red-throated loon looks, and is, awkward on land. Its legs are set far back on its body—perfect for flying, but not for walking. In fact, the bird uses its breast to push its way over the ground! This type of movement would look even clumsier if not for the fact that this species is the smallest of all loons. Perhaps because of its small size, the red-throated loon is the only type of loon that is able to fly from land; other loons must take off from water. Once in the air, all loons are fast, powerful fliers.

Loons are most at home in water. Their bodies are streamlined, with large feet that have webs between the front toes. Loons are excellent divers. They catch their food underwater, grasping it with their bill. Their diet consists mainly of fish, but also includes shrimp, snails, and water insects.

Like other loons, the red-throated variety migrates with the seasons, spending the summer on small ponds in the far north, and flying south in the fall. It winters on bays and other coastal waters and returns to its northern habitat in spring.

Red-throated loons mate and nest on land, near the water's edge. The female lays two dark, spotted eggs. The parents take turns incubating the eggs, which hatch in about four weeks. The babies are born covered with soft down feathers. They can swim within a day of hatching, but they cannot fly until they are about two months old.

Slow Loris
Nycticebus coucang

Length: 10 to 15 inches
Length of the Tail: up to 2 inches
Weight: ½ to 3½ pounds
Diet: fruit and insects

Number of Young: 1
Home: Southeast Asia
Order: Primates
Family: Lorises and pottos

 Rain forests

 Mammals

© D. HARING / OSF / ANIMALS ANIMALS / EARTH SCENES

The slow loris looks much like a teddy bear, but it is actually a primate, the order that includes apes, monkeys, and humans. This creature is chubby, with a round head and small ears that are almost hidden in its dense fur. Its short front and back legs are nearly the same length, and its tail is very short and stumpy.

The slow loris is well named. Its name is believed to come from either a Dutch or a Flemish word that means "slow" or "lazy." The slow loris moves very, very slowly. It is active at night, when it looks for food in treetops. Powerful muscles in the loris's hands allow the creature to grip branches and hold on to tree bark for long periods of time. The slightest sound will cause the slow loris to stop, or "freeze." It remains motionless, often for several hours, until there are no more signs of danger. The slow loris sleeps during the day. Asleep, it looks like a ball of fur. Its head is tucked underneath its arms, close to its belly. This position helps prevent the loss of body heat.

A newborn slow loris is covered with fur. During the first few days of its life, it clings to its mother's belly. Then the mother leaves the baby on a tree branch, well protected from predators, and goes off to find food. When she returns in the morning, the mother picks up the young one and shares her food with it.

Atlantic Mackerel
Scomber scombrus

Length: up to 22 inches
Diet: small crustaceans, worms, and fish
Number of Eggs: up to 500,000

Weight: up to 7½ pounds
Home: North Atlantic Ocean
Order: Perchlike fishes
Family: Mackerel and tuna

 Oceans and Shores

 Fish

Atlantic mackerel migrate with the seasons. During warm weather, they live in large groups called schools or shoals. They swim rapidly just beneath the surface of the sea, where they feed on animal plankton. The mackerel's favorite food at this time is small crustaceans. Sometimes fishermen catch mackerel whose stomachs are packed with crustaceans, which the fishermen call "red feed."

In winter, Atlantic mackerel live in gullies on the ocean floor. They are not very active during this time. They do not eat much, and their diet is varied. They feed on shrimp and other smaller crustaceans, bristle worms, and small fish.

Atlantic mackerel spawn in spring and early summer. A female lays hundreds of thousands of eggs. Each egg contains a tiny droplet of oil. The oil keeps the egg floating near the surface of the ocean. Many of the eggs die or are eaten by predators. Eggs that survive hatch in about four days. Young mackerel grow rapidly. By the time they are two years old, they are 12 to 13 inches long. After that, they grow much more slowly. If they are not eaten by tuna, sharks, or other enemies, they can live to about 20 years of age.

Mackerel are very important food fish and are sold fresh or canned. Most of the mackerel caught by fishermen are 14 to 18 inches long and weigh less than 1 pound.

Mandrill
Papio sphinx

Length: 25 to 30 inches
Weight: up to 55 pounds
Diet: fruit, shoots, and insects
Number of Young: 1

Home: West Africa
Order: Primates
Family: Macaques, baboons, and monkeys

 Rain forests

 Mammals

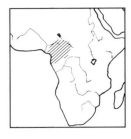

 Endangered Animals

© JOHN GUISTINA / BRUCE COLEMAN INC.

Once you have seen a mandrill at the zoo, you will never forget it! This large baboon from the African tropical forest has unique bright red and blue colors on its nose and buttocks. Its turned-up nose and nostrils are bright red. Blue ridges on each side of the red areas make the face seem like a Halloween mask. Colors of this "mask" are much brighter in the male than in the female. The bright colors allow people to see the mandrill in the dense forest. Scientists think that these marks, which get brighter when the animal is angry, are used to frighten other animals. They are particularly helpful to the larger males when they want to prove to the young ones that they are the boss.

Mandrills live on the ground most of the time. They roam in the forest on four legs, looking for food from daybreak to noon and then, after a rest, until sunset. Some lift stones and dead branches to uncover insects; others pick grains, look for mushrooms, or collect fruit. Finally, at dusk, they climb up trees to spend the night.

Although they are rather sweet and mild in captivity, mandrills are quite frightening in the wild. When an adult mandrill opens its mouth wide and shows it large upper canine teeth, even leopards avoid it. Because of the destruction of the forests, the mandrill has been on the endangered species list since 1980.

Pacific Manta
Manta hamiltoni

Weight: up to 3,500 pounds
Diet: plankton
Method of Reproduction:
  young hatch from eggs within
  the mother and are born alive

Width and Wingspan: up to
  20 feet
Home: Pacific Ocean
Order: Rays and their relatives
Family: Mantas

 Oceans and Shores

 Fish

© JEFF ROTMAN / PHOTO RESEARCHERS

Some people think that the Pacific manta looks like a giant bat. Others think it resembles a tent. The name for this fish actually comes from a Spanish word that means "blanket." At one time, pearl divers and other swimmer feared these large, "winged" fish. They believed that mantas attacked people, and that a manta swimming overhead would cover them with its wings and then eat them. This superstition, as well as the manta's hornlike snout, led to the common name "devil ray." Actually, mantas are usually harmless to people, although they may become dangerous when harpooned.

The Pacific manta is truly the graceful giant of the ocean. It has a flat body with a long, thin tail. Wide, winglike fins are attached to the front of the head. A manta uses these fins to guide food into its mouth. As the manta swims through masses of plankton at the water's surface, the flapping fins set up currents that sweep the plankton toward the mouth. Pacific mantas are filter-feeders; a special structure in the throat acts as a strainer, keeping the food in the mouth until the manta is ready to swallow. Water can pass through the strainer to the gills, carrying needed oxygen so the manta does not suffocate. The Pacific manta has teeth only in its lower jaw. These teeth are very small, and they are arranged in rows.

42

Marabou
Leptoptilos crumeniferus

Length: 4 feet
Wingspan: 10 feet
Diet: carrion and small animals
Number of Eggs: 2 to 5

Home: eastern and central Africa
Order: Storks and spoonbills
Family: Storks

 Fresh Water

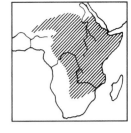

 Birds

© ALISSA CRANDALL / CORBIS

In the African savanna, a vast plain scattered with low trees, the body of the dead zebra is warmed by the morning sun. Soon, huge wings glide above it; first vultures arrive, and then the marabous appear. Their meal is ready. They will feed on anything they can find—frogs, rodents, and even small crocodiles that they kill with their powerful beaks.

Even if they do not look alike, the marabou and the beautiful stork are close relatives. The marabou does not appear to have a neck. It has an enormous feathered pouch, or bag, hanging from its neck down over its breast. The head is almost bare.

Marabous are found almost everywhere in Africa, except in the desert and in West Africa. They also live in cities, where they raid trash cans. The marabou's taste in food is actually quite useful: It disposes of dead animals on the outskirts of the cities.

Marabous make their large nests in trees, often near a watering hole. The male and female take turns sitting on the eggs for 35 days. They feed their young by eating the food first, then spitting it up directly into the nest within reach of their young. The young birds can fly when they are about four months old. The marabou is clumsy on the ground but beautiful in flight. Its large wings, when opened, can spread to 10 feet and carry this heavy bird high in the sky.

Margay
Felis wiedii

Length of the Body: 21 to 32 inches
Length of the Tail: 13 to 20 inches
Weight: 7 to 20 pounds
Diet: birds and small mammals

Number of Young: 1 or 2
Home: North, Central, and South America
Order: Carnivores
Family: Cats

 Forests and Mountains

 Mammals

? Endangered Animals

© TOM BRAKEFIELD / CORBIS

In the 1800s a wildcat called the margay roamed as far north as New Mexico and southern Texas. Today there is some doubt as to the survival of these populations. Margays can still be found to the south, in the mountains and tropical rain forests from Mexico through Brazil. But this elegant cat is endangered throughout its range. The two main threats are hunting and the destruction of its habitat.

Each year, fur traders around the world sell thousands of margay pelts. The cat's spotted cinnamon fur is used as expensive collars and in hats. At the same time, people continue to destroy the margay's wilderness home for lumber and land development.

Of all the cats in the world, the margay may be the most skillful and acrobatic tree climber. The margay's wide paws are flexible, like hands, and give the cat an exceptionally firm grip. It can scurry up and down a tree trunk like a squirrel, with its head facing downward. (Other cats must clumsily back down, tailfirst.) The margay can even hang upside down from a branch, using the unusually long claws on its back feet for support. The agile margay hunts at night, silently nabbing unsuspecting birds and squirrels in their nests. If it cannot grab its prey by surprise, the margay gives a tremendous chase, leaping and scrambling from tree to tree.